A PLACE
CALLED
ACCEPTANCE

Ministry with

Families of

Children with

Disabilities

May your church be known as "a place called acceptance!"

Kathleen Deyer Bolduc

BRIDGE
resources

Louisville, Kentucky

© 2001 Kathleen Deyer Bolduc

Unless otherwise noted, Scripture quotations are from the
New Revised Standard Version of the Bible, copyright © 1989
by the Division of Christian Education of the National Council
of the Churches of Christ in the U.S.A. Used by permission.

Every effort has been made to trace copyrights on the
materials included in this book. If any copyrighted material
has nevertheless been included without permission and due
acknowledgment, proper credit will be inserted in future
printings after notice has been received.

The quotation on page 7 is taken from *The Broken Body* by
Jean Vanier, published and copyright 1988 by Darton
Longman and Todd Ltd. and used by permission of the
publishers.

Edited by Cassandra D. Williams

Book interior and cover design by Eric Morrell

Cover photo by Heidi Helm

First edition

Published by Bridge Resources
Louisville, Kentucky

Web site address: http://www.bridgeresources.org

PRINTED IN THE UNITED STATES OF AMERICA

01 02 03 04 05 06 07 08 09 10 —10 9 8 7 6 5 4 3 2 1

Library of Congress Cataloging-in-Publication Data
Bolduc, Kathleen Deyer, date.
    A place called acceptance : ministry with families of
    children with disabilities /
Kathleen Deyer Bolduc.— 1st ed.
        p. cm.
    Includes bibliographical references.
    ISBN 1-57895-098-8 (alk. paper)
      1. Parents of handicapped children—Religious life.
    2. Church work with families. I. Title.
    BV4596.P35 B65 2001
    259'.4—dc21   2001043161

Contents

Acknowledgments

This book would not have been possible without the encouragement and support of several organizations and people.

The College of Mount St. Joseph, Cincinnati, Ohio: This book began as an integrating project for completion of a master's degree in religious studies. I am indebted to the entire staff of the Religious and Pastoral Family Studies Department, particularly Dr. Alan deCourcy, who served as my advisor on this project. Thank you for giving me the opportunity to focus my studies on something so dear to my own heart, and for expanding my horizons far beyond my own family experience.

The Writing Academy: For seventeen years, this organization has been a source of teaching, inspiration, and fellowship. Blessings to all of you!

Cassandra Williams, my editor at Bridge Resources: Casey, you have been a joy to work with. Thank you for giving me a forum not once, but twice, to share the lessons I've learned as the mother of a very special young man named Joel.

Bonnie Shuman, fellow traveler: Thanks for always being there when I need you.

My husband, Wally: Hugs to you for walking alongside me every step of the way, and to my sons Matt, Justin, and Joel. I love you!

I dedicate this book to Carol Schubert, Joel's Sunday school teacher; to her husband Bob, Joel's big buddy; and to the Tuesday Night Prayer Group, which has faithfully surrounded our family with prayer. All of you truly have made College Hill Presbyterian Church "a place called acceptance" for Joel and our family. You are appreciated and loved beyond measure!

Introduction

Imagine, just for a moment, that someone you love has died, throwing you into a time of mourning more intense than anything you've ever experienced. Your emotions, like pinball marbles, bounce from denial to anger, from fear to confusion, from sadness to disbelief, from frustration to guilt to depression. And your spiritual life? It, too, suffers, as you bounce between praising God for the gift this person was to you, and one-sided screaming matches with God.

You wrestle with this alone until it finally dawns on you. You are part of a church community! Surely, you can find some help there. So you make an appointment with your pastor. You explain your situation. A loved one has died. You are confused and lost and afraid. You need help.

Your pastor listens closely. She says she's very sorry for your loss. But, she continues, no one else in this particular church has experienced the death of a loved one. The entire church is as confused as you by this sudden loss. The perfect solution would be for you, the grieving one, to teach a class on grieving for the congregation! Let them know what you're experiencing. Lead a support group for people of other churches who have gone through similar trials. And in the sharing, who knows, perhaps you will experience healing!

This scenario may seem farfetched, but I've experienced it as the mother of my son, Joel, who has multiple handicapping conditions. Countless other parents of children with disabilities have experienced it as well. It happens in big churches as well as small; in churches with excellent staffs and good people in the pews. Of course, the presenting problem was not the grief that comes with the physical death of a loved one, but the grief that accompanies the death of a dream: the loss of the dreamed-of child so eagerly anticipated through nine long months of pregnancy; of the child whom it was assumed would negotiate the stages of childhood, adolescence, and adulthood in a typical fashion.

When children are born with a disability, or are disabled from illness or accident, parents grieve. Not only do they grieve, they also face extraordinary pressures on top of the normal stresses and strains that are part and parcel of the parenting experience. And yet, these families are often overlooked within the ministries of our churches. Too often, parents themselves are expected to spearhead any ministry efforts that would allow their child to participate in the life of the church community.

This book was born while I was doing graduate work in the field of religious and pastoral family studies at the College of Mount St. Joseph. I spent one of the three years of the program in concentrated study on disability, its effect on the family system, and the role of the church in ministering with families of children with disabilities. My purpose in writing it is twofold. First is to provide a "wake-up call" to those in leadership positions within the church. Families of children with disabilities have a deep need for compassion and acceptance, as well as for practical assistance, from their church families. In a world that judges a person's worth on physical attributes and accomplishment, these families desperately need a place to belong; a place that will love and embrace their children just as they are, regardless of physical, cognitive, or behavioral disabilities. This book is also meant to be an educational tool. Within its pages you will find many practical ministry suggestions, as well as resources that will be helpful in beginning or augmenting a ministry with children who have disabilities and with their families.

Some of the information in this book flows directly out of my experiences as Joel's mother and as an active lay leader in the Presbyterian

Church (U.S.A.). At fifteen years, Joel is cognitively on a preschool level, and has many autistic-like tendencies as well as an anxiety disorder. Learning new skills and coping with environmental overload are constant challenges for my son. Living with Joel's challenging behavior is a daily reality for me, as well as for the rest of my family.

My prayer is that by piecing together research on disability, family systems theory, and the church with my own personal story, the dry bones of factual information will assume human form—for disability always takes on human form. Our society, in its tendency to categorize and label, often forgets this. It is easier to dismiss that "poor mentally retarded boy" than to see the promise and gift of the child within.

Joel, as cognitively impaired as he is, has proven to be a powerful agent of transformation in my life. I do not pretend that life with Joel has been easy. Disability is never easy. Life with Joel has stretched me at times beyond that which I thought myself capable. As a friend of mine, a mother of a child with Down Syndrome once said, "I kept praying for God to change my son, but he changed me instead." Because of Joel I now have eyes that see how persons with disabilities have been marginalized and disenfranchised within the church, a heart that is beginning to fathom the depth of the love of God, and ears that hear the call of God to reach out in welcome to families that live with disability.

My prayer is that through the study of this book your congregation will become more welcoming, more accepting, more supportive of children with disabilities and of their families.

1 | Prologue

The Invitation
A Poem for Two Voices

A party!
The Church is throwing a party!
Prepare the guest list.
Pen the invitations.
Send them to every Christian in the neighborhood,
regardless of denomination.
Hand-deliver to those with wealth and prestige . . .
the ones with the means to help us to grow!

Go, buy the food and wine!
the finest fruit . . .
the freshest vegetables . . .
the best cuts of meat . . .
the most expensive vintages of wine.

Ready the table!
Lay it with fine linens,
Set it with silver, crystal and china.
Call the florist.
Summon the musicians.
Stringed instruments and trained soloists,
music to praise our Lord
for all that the Lord has done for us!

A sumptuous feast!
A celebration of the senses!

A commemoration of Christ's presence among us!

Invite the outcasts

What's that you say?
Invite the . . . who?

The poor
The maimed
The lame
The blind

You must be kidding!
We're talking first class here . . .
Why . . . they wouldn't know how to act!
They couldn't appreciate the excellence!
Only the best for . . . our Lord, is that you?

Oh no, we would never forget you, Lord!

Yes. Did you forget?

I know that, dear ones.
But did you forget that if one member suffers, all suffer?
If one member is honored, all rejoice?
Weakness in strength
Strength in weakness

When you put it like that . . .
I suppose we could re-think our guest list . . .
Perhaps we could re-word our invitations . . .
but I insist on calligraphy!
Only the best . . .

Isaiah 61 would make
the perfect invitation

I don't know as I remember that Scripture.
Could you refresh our memories?

The spirit of the Lord God
is upon me because the Lord
has anointed me to bring
good tidings to the afflicted,
to bind up the brokenhearted,
to proclaim liberty to the
captives and the opening of the
prison to those who are bound

Forget the mailing list!
Scrap the formal invitations!
Go into the streets,
the prisons,
the group homes,
the hospitals and psychiatric wards,
the parks where the homeless sleep,
where the least of these are languishing for love . . .

The body of Christ is throwing a party!

2 | Musings on Disability and Theology

Theology not only deals with disability. Theology is disability. It is the impossible science of the supernatural, the search for the "law of God," the knowing of the unknowable, trying to see the infinite through our nearsighted lenses.[1]

Genesis 1:26–27 reads:
Then God said, "Let us make humankind in our image, according to our likeness; and let them have dominion over the fish of the sea, and over the birds of the air, and over the cattle, and over all the wild animals of the earth, and over every creeping thing that creeps upon the earth." So God created humankind in his image, in the image of God he created them; male and female he created them.

Imagine reading the Creation story, believing it with all of your heart, soul, and mind, never stopping to wonder exactly what it means to be created "in God's image." The words sound good and true, and as we gaze into the eyes of loved ones, there is no reason to question too deeply the meaning behind the familiar words.

Then an expectant mother goes into labor. She wrestles, rides, and ultimately endures waves of pain more intense than any she has ever experienced—a rending of flesh, a tearing and splitting apart of the very fabric of her body.

A child is born.

The woman's own flesh and blood, carried within her body for nine long months. Her very own child, so often dreamed of, so eagerly anticipated. In the wake of this precious new life, pain mysteriously recedes and disappears. Joy swallows agony, digests and spits it out, as she reaches hungrily for her newborn child.

But wait. Why is the baby blue and gasping for breath?

Why doesn't he suck strongly, pummeling her breast with tiny fists?

Why, when she takes her home, does she not develop according to schedule?

Something is wrong with this mother's child, this precious baby, so long awaited. The father stands by, helpless, his role as guardian and general fixer-of-all-broken-things obliterated. Joy no longer runs and jumps through the upstairs hallway. Depression and desperation take up residence in the spare rooms of their souls.

This is where disability and theology collide: in the crucible of grief as parents face the bitter fact of a child's disabling condition.

Why? Why my child? Why me? What kind of God allows a child to be born blind, or deaf, or with mental retardation or spina bifida? Does this have anything to do with sin? Retribution? Judgment? Or does this mean there is no God, that life is one long, meaningless, bad joke? Would a loving God use a helpless child as an object lesson in grace? What does it mean to be "created in the image of God"? Parents of children with disabilities wrestle with these questions, and all too often, they struggle in isolation.

I would like to be able to say that the corporate body of Christ, the Church with a capital C, has been an invaluable support to me and my family throughout our journey with our son Joel, who has mental retardation and autism spectrum disorder. Unfortunately, this has not always been the case . . . and from many conversations I've had over the years with other families in similar situations, this is more the norm than the exception.

In the early stages of my grief, in my personal struggle to reconcile Joel's disability with my belief in a loving God, I found my greatest comfort not among God's people, but in the Scriptures. As I sought a better understanding of who God is, and why he would allow a beautiful boy to be born with a damaged brain, I searched the Bible and found God's nature to be one of loving kindness, compassion, justice, and mercy. The Psalms were especially helpful to me, as they echoed my heart cry of grief. *Are you there, God? Do you care, God?* The answer, repeated time and again, was sure: "When the righteous cry for help, the Lord hears, and rescues them from all their troubles. The Lord is near to the brokenhearted, and saves the crushed in spirit. Many are the afflictions of the righteous, but the Lord rescues them all" (Ps. 34:17–19).

Reading the Prophets, I found that God possesses an unquenchable desire for justice and mercy. This desire began to well up within my own heart as I witnessed again and again the ramifications of living with disability in this culture: pity, condescension, marginalization, and rejection. How I hung on to these words from Micah 6:8: "What does the Lord require of you but to do justice, and to love kindness, and to walk humbly with your God?" and Isaiah 61:1–3: "The spirit of the Lord God is upon me, because

the Lord has anointed me; he has sent me to bring good news to the oppressed, to bind up the brokenhearted, to proclaim liberty to the captives, and release to the prisoners; to proclaim the year of the Lord's favor, and the day of vengeance of our God; to comfort all who mourn; to provide for those who mourn in Zion—to give them a garland instead of ashes, the oil of gladness instead of mourning, the mantle of praise instead of a faint spirit. They will be called oaks of righteousness, the planting of the Lord, to display his glory." These powerful words reveal what God desires for Joel, and for all of those who live with broken bodies, hearts, or minds. According to the Gospel of Luke, Jesus Christ, the invisible God made visible, is the fulfillment of Isaiah's prophecy. Fully human, yet fully God, his earthly ministry reveals God's priorities: release for the captives, sight for the blind, liberty for the oppressed.

What is it that holds us captive, that which oppresses us? Very often we are enslaved by cultural belief systems. In Jesus' culture, those with disabilities were relegated to the margins of society. Our culture's preoccupation with perfection, beauty, and power has led many to believe that those who do not measure up mentally or physically are somehow inferior; that those who differ greatly from the norm are somehow unworthy. I believe it is these very belief systems from which Jesus wants to free us.

Kahlil Gibran writes, "Your pain is the breaking of the shell that encloses your understanding."[2] The pain I experienced as I grieved Joel's disability broke open the Scriptures for me. I came to understand that Jesus turns upside down the cultural belief that brokenness is to be avoided at all costs. Christ challenged me to face and embrace my brokenness as well as Joel's brokenness, so that God's power might be released within both of us. I began to trust Jesus Christ to tell me what it means to be a child of God, rather than accept society's definition of personhood. I began to trust Jesus to tell me the worth of my son Joel, as well as my worth as Joel's mother.

It is in Jesus' relationships that we see the depth of his love manifested. The oppressed, the disenfranchised, the sick, and the broken—

these were the people he surrounded himself with. Jesus was a boundary breaker. Through his love and acceptance Jesus broke through the barriers that separated those he touched from their deepest selves, and thus the barrier between themselves and a loving God. In his ability to pierce to the very core of a person, Jesus swept away years of hopelessness in a single meeting. Healing meant much more than physical restoration. It included emotional and spiritual healing and enabled transformation to take place.

In the story of the Last Supper, Jesus provides a living metaphor for the kind of love he requires. He takes off his outer garment, girds himself with a towel, and kneels to wash the disciples' feet. When he is finished, he returns to the table and says, "'Do you know what I have done to you? You call me Teacher and Lord—and you are right, for that is what I am. So if I, your Lord and Teacher, have washed your feet, you also ought to wash one another's feet. For I have set you an example, that you also should do as I have done to you'" (John 13:3–5; 12–15). Jean Vanier, founder of the L'Arche communities for persons with cognitive disabilities, writes of the deeply symbolic nature of Jesus' actions.

> During his last paschal meal
> Jesus goes even further
> in his mission to meet and love people,
> to touch them.
> He takes water in a basin and a towel.
> He stoops down and washes the feet
> of each one of his disciples.
> He no longer addresses their intelligence,
> their heads,
> but bends down lower than they
> to wash what is lowest and dirtiest
> what is closest to the earth:
> he washes their feet . . .
> So Jesus begins to make the passage
> from the one who is healer
> to the one who is wounded;
> from a man of compassion
> to the man in need of compassion . . .
> From announcing the good news to the poor, Jesus becomes the poor.

He crosses over the boundary line of humanity which separates those whose needs are satisfied from those who are broken and cry out in need.[3]

The theme becoming clear here is that of a God who lives among us, walks alongside us, suffers with us, rejoices with us—a God who is as comfortable with those who live with disability as with those who are of sound body and mind. What a comfort in light of our own vulnerability and our own fragility. Vanier believes that in identifying himself with the suffering of humanity, Jesus builds a bridge so that communion with God may occur, and thus, paradoxically, liberation. The suffering itself may not disappear, but the ability to live with it is gifted to the sufferer.

In the resource *That All May Enter: Responding to People with Disability Concerns,* it is stated that as human beings, we are created in God's image and are called to be God's ministers, that we are frail and vulnerable beings, that Christ addresses us in our strength as well as in our weakness. It is not only our responsibility but also our opportunity to reach out to one another in times of need to strengthen and to heal.

> *Our contemporary society has a special need for the ministry of the handicapped and to the handicapped. As the church learns to recognize human weakness-in-strength and strength-in weakness, it begins to discover the cost and joy of discipleship. It finds that the sharing of burdens is the sharing of opportunities. It witnesses to God's gracious love.*[4]

That All May Worship: An Interfaith Welcome to People with Disabilities (5th ed., Washington, D.C.: The National Organization on Disability, 1997), a common-sense, how-to guide for congregations that are seeking to make all persons feel welcomed, regardless of ability level, strongly proclaims the message that the house of God is to be open to everyone.

When we talk about welcoming people with disabilities into the church, we often ask, "How can we minister to people with developmental or physical disabilities?" This is a good question, but I would suggest we first ask a different question: "What can those with disabilities bring to a community of faith?" or put more concretely, "Can persons with mental retardation, cerebral palsy, or autism minister to our faith communities?"

Joel brings many gifts to his relationships, as has been discovered to the delight of those in the church who have befriended him. He brings unconditional love, spontaneity, enthusiasm, genuine affection and concern, simplicity of spirit, and a love for worship and praise. Those with physical disabilities bring the same variety of gifts of the Spirit as our able-bodied members bring. Many of them also bring a gut-level understanding that a person's worth has nothing to do with the outer packaging. These qualities would strengthen any community, be it church, family, or neighborhood.

Perhaps we fear those with disabilities because they are an all too-real reminder of our own fragility. In 2 Corinthians 4:7, Paul writes of our common fragility as human beings: "But we have this treasure in clay jars, so that it may be clear that this extraordinary power belongs to God and does not come from us." Disabilities are simply a normal outcome of the living process. As clay jars, each one of us is vulnerable to accident, illness, and the ravages of time. According to Mary Jane Owen, executive director of the National Catholic Office for People with Disabilities, a powerful community is formed when we truly accept one another, frailties and all.

When I really acknowledge that I am in need of help, I become more civilized because I need to relate to you. And when you become aware, and your children become aware, and our society becomes aware, and our parish becomes aware, truly on a gut level, as well as on a head level and a spiritual level, that we need each other, what have we formed? We've formed a powerful sense of community. It binds us together. Your needs, your strengths; my needs, my strengths. Together, those intertwining threads weave the strongest fabric of society, of church, of community.[5]

Jesus calls us, as his church, to struggle against a powerful secular belief system that judges a person's worth on his or her accomplishments or physical and mental attributes. As we worship the risen Christ, we must remember the wounded Christ and never lose sight of the enormous gift of grace given as God took on the disability of human form. Let us follow Jesus' example and become boundary breakers, toppling down barriers of fear, ignorance, and prejudice as we minister alongside brothers and sisters—children and adult alike—with disabilities.

So we do not lose heart. Even though our outer nature is wasting away, our inner nature is being renewed day by day. For this slight momentary affliction is preparing us for an eternal weight of glory beyond all measure, because we look not at what can be seen but at what cannot be seen; for what can be seen is temporary, but what cannot be seen is eternal.
(2 Cor. 4:16–18)

Notes
1. Thomas Orrin Bentz, "Theology in Disability," *Grapevine* 13, no. 5 (November 1981): 2.
2. Kahlil Gibran, *The Prophet* (New York: Alfred A. Knopf, 1979), 52.
3. Jean Vanier, *The Broken Body* (London: Darton Longman and Todd, 1988), pp. 47–49.
4. *That All May Enter: Responding to People with Disability Concerns* (Louisville, Ky.: Office of the General Assembly and the Education and Congregational Nurture Ministry Unit, Presbyterian Church (U.S.A.), 1989), 11.
5. Mary Jane Owen, *Disability Ministry: Perspectives on Disability*, produced by Marilyn E. Bishop (Dayton, Ohio: Center for Ministry with Disabled People, University of Dayton), videocassette.

3 | The Wasteland of Grief

When a child has a disability, parents grieve, but they grieve differently. Even in this most intimate relationship, marriage, we are often isolated in our grief. What's happening inside us is too terrible to tell, too awful to show. The guilt. The rage. The helplessness. The doubt of self, of God.[1]

Journeying through the wasteland of grief is lonely. I know. I've traveled this land for fifteen years, since the birth of my third son, Joel Christopher. Joel has moderate mental retardation, autistic tendencies, and has recently been diagnosed with an anxiety disorder. As Joel's mother, I travel a rocky road. A road strewn with boulders of denial. A road that has brought me to my knees in prayer. It is a winding road, and its curves surprise me one day with anger, the next with joy. Occasionally the way is damp and foggy, covered with clouds of depression. But I keep on trudging, climbing over obstacles and skirting boulders with one destination in mind.

Somewhere along this journey lies a place called acceptance.

When Joel was finally diagnosed, at age five, with moderate mental retardation, the grieving process raced along at full speed. Forced out of denial, my husband and I moved at varying speeds into bargaining, anger, and depression. Today Joel is fifteen, and he continually teaches us lessons in love, acceptance, patience, and trust as we move toward acceptance of his handicapping condition.

STAGES OF GRIEF EXPERIENCED BY PARENTS OF CHILDREN WITH DISABILITIES

"God must have chosen you to parent this very special child because God knew that you were strong enough and loving enough to handle her." How often words like these are thoughtlessly spoken by well-meaning family and friends when a family discovers their child is deaf or blind, has spina bifida, mental retardation, autism, or multiple handicaps. Parents may come to believe they were chosen by God for this demanding task in the years to come, after the grief work is done, but at the time of diagnosis, and oftentimes for years afterward, fear, anger, despair, frustration, guilt, depression, and denial are the order of the day. Reconciling the idea of a loving God with the pain of their situation is almost blasphemous.

Parents of children with disabilities ride a roller coaster of emotions as they attempt to gain their bearings in a world turned topsy-turvy by disability. Disability is a word shrouded in fear and mystery; a word every expectant mother secretly fears; a word every loving parent dreads. Disability is a subject with which many people have no experience. Disability is something we want to believe happens only to other people, other children, other families. Parents of children with disabilities intimately know the wasteland of grief. When disability strikes at birth, parents grieve the loss of a dream—the loss of the child for whom they had spent countless hours planning. When disability strikes later in a child's life, due to accident or illness, parents grieve the loss of the child they already knew and loved so well. In either case, parents are plunged into a time of mourning that closely corresponds to the grief surrounding the death of a loved one.

The five stages of grief identified by Elizabeth Kubler Ross in her landmark book *On Death and Dying* (New York: MacMillan, 1969) can be loosely employed as a rubric for understanding the grief experienced by parents of children with disabilities. They are: denial, anger, bargaining, depression, and acceptance.

Denial

Denial is a defense mechanism that allows parents time to assimilate the impact the child's disability will have upon their lives, the life of the family, and the life of the child. Parents may spend months, or even years, making the rounds of specialist after specialist, looking for someone to tell them it isn't true; that it isn't as bad as it once sounded; that there is a cure or medication or therapy that will make everything better. A period of denial is typical, becoming unhealthy only if it is chronic in nature. It is not unusual for feelings of fear to be present in this stage of grief; fear of the unknown, fear of ambivalent feelings toward the child, fear of not being able to meet the child's needs.

In my own journey toward acceptance, denial was like a quicksand that sucked me in and wouldn't let me go. When Joel was two years old and not yet walking, his physical

therapist recommended we enroll him in a multihandicapped preschool in our district. My reaction was one of terror.

> *Multihandicapped! The word hit me like a physical blow. I gasped. The curtain I had hung to protect me from my worst fears had been lifted. Silent words formed. Angry words. Fearful words. My child is not handicapped! Don't you dare use those words in the same sentence with my son's name! Developmentally delayed yes, but multihandicapped, never! No! No! No![2]*

Anger

When reality seeps through the denial, anger is often the result, accompanied by feelings of resentment and even rage. Anger is one of the most frightening emotions we face as human beings, and also one of the most socially unacceptable. The anger may be aimed outward in words of blame—it's the doctor's fault, the hospital's fault, the anesthesiologist's fault. Parents may direct their anger toward God for allowing the disability. They may direct it toward their spouse, or even toward the child.

Robert Naseef, the father of a son with autism, is a psychologist who specializes in working with families of children with disabilities. He writes of his guilt over the anger he felt toward his son, Tariq.

> *In my case, Tariq was five before I was able to admit to myself that I was angry at him. He was simply not who I wanted him to be. Even now I am uncomfortable acknowledging this. It feels like a defect in me, a flaw that I would rather hide if I could. Isn't a parent's love for a child supposed to be unconditional?[3]*

Guilt

Anger may also be turned inward where it manifests itself as self-blame, guilt, and shame. This is where the "if onlys" get the better of us: If only I'd eaten better food when I was pregnant. If only I'd exercised more, or exercised less. If only I had made better choices with drugs and alcohol when I was in college. If only I'd gone to church more—argued with God less—spent more time praying.

While guilt usually involves a bad feeling around something we did or didn't do, shame involves a painful feeling of unworthiness of our personhood, regardless of our actions. When a child does not fit the world's mold, a parent's sense of self may be violated, and feelings of incompetence, weakness, and powerlessness may arise. These feelings are generally unconscious, and leave a person puzzled as to their origin. For most of us, our children mirror in some way our expectations for ourselves, and when our sons or daughters do not "measure up," it is our own person who is found lacking.

Beth Kephart, author of the beautiful memoir *A Slant of Sun: One Child's Courage,* writes of the self-doubt that plagued her as she strove to break down the boundaries surrounding her son Jeremy, who had been diagnosed with pervasive developmental disorder.

> *It seems to me that my inability to enter my son's world is a personal failure, a crisis. I do not mention it to the few friends who call. I hide it from my family, and I decline to talk about such things with my husband, who somehow always understands where Jeremy's cars are going and why; knows, just by observing, which car is the odd car out and free for moving. I can't talk to my husband because he is the better parent, and so in the dark at night, I lie awake and wonder, worry about the instincts I am lacking, and conclude—horrified—that love alone may not be enough.*[4]

Again, fear may play a major part in this stage: fear of what is not understood; fear for the child's future; fear of society's treatment of the child. Uncertainty looms larger than life, bringing with it paralysis.

Bargaining

Bargaining is that stage in which parents make pacts with God: If you heal my child I will never miss church again; I will do whatever you ask of

me; I will be the world's best mother (or father). Some parents bargain with themselves, believing that if they just spend more time looking for the right doctors, reading the right books, or working with their child in the correct way the disability will "get better."

I have known parents who put the remainder of their lives on hold as they pour themselves exclusively into their special child. Marriage, other siblings in the family, and job become secondary concerns to the overwhelming task of "healing" the child's disability through occupational and physical therapy, medication, the right school program, and so on.

Depression

Depression occurs when the loss of the dream of "what might have been" begins to seep through the denial and anger. The depression may manifest itself physically, in aches, pains, fatigue, poor digestion, an inability to sleep, or a desire to do nothing but sleep. Routine chores become overwhelming, and activities that once brought pleasure are either performed by rote or avoided all together. The depression that affects one person physically may affect another as simply a dull acceptance that the situation is not going to change, that the disability is a reality and that it will never "go away."

It is not at all unusual for depression to affect men and women in different ways. In my own marriage, depression manifested itself in angry words and a flurry of activity for my husband. For me, it became harder and harder to get out of bed in the mornings; keeping up with the daily household chores became overwhelming; and tears, rather than angry words, were in abundant supply. When feelings of depression are severe or prolonged, professional help, in the form of counseling or medication, may be indicated.

Acceptance

Eventually, the intensity of anger and depression will subside, making pacts with God and self diminishes, and parents begin to move into acceptance. Acceptance is a time of dreaming new dreams for the child, and building on the child's strengths. It is a time of making plans and being realistic about what can be done. It is also a time of moving out of isolation—of seeking help from extended family, the church, friends, and professionals. In some ways, this is the hardest stage, as it requires imagination, courage, strength, and action.

THE PROCESS OF GRIEF

Professionals have found that the most crucial time in the lives of parents of children with disabilities is from the time they receive a diagnosis of disability until they learn what courses of action are open to them. This time interval is characteristically one of intense emotional upheaval, while the parents attempt to reorganize their lives around the fact of the disabling condition.

Parents of children with disabilities also know what has been called chronic grief. Acceptance is not a static state, but a process that continues throughout the life-cycle of the child. Guilt, shame, denial, depression, and anger may resurface and need to be worked through as a child becomes a preschooler, approaches elementary school age, and then moves on to adolescence and young adulthood. Acceptance does not mean parents no longer look for or pray for a cure, but that, having worked through the grief, they begin to accept their children as they are, to appreciate their strengths and tolerate their weaknesses, and to genuinely take pleasure in them. The child becomes simply another piece of the family system puzzle.

It is important to realize that these stages are not necessarily traveled in sequence nor are they experienced the same by everyone. Denial, anger, bargaining, depression, and acceptance come and go, in no particular order, each capable of resurfacing at any time. One person may deny his child's disability for years, while his spouse moves back and forth among all the stages. Another may get stuck in anger and spend great amounts of energy venting that anger toward God, her child, her husband, or herself. Yet another may forge ahead through all the stages and reach the point of acceptance quickly.

It is also important to note that each of these stages serves a purpose and makes a positive contribution to the life of the grieving parent. Denial protects us from a reality we are not yet ready to face, giving us time to marshal the inner resources that we need. Anger energizes, gives us the drive and ambition to work long hours with our children; to prove the experts wrong; to make more money to pay for therapy; or to afford special schools. And depression, as frightening and consuming as it can be, takes us deep down to a place where we finally come to understand what Kahlil Gibran meant when he wrote, "Your joy is your sorrow unmasked. The deeper that sorrow carves into your being, the more joy you can contain."[5]

Parents need help working through the grief process both as they work toward a diagnosis and after the diagnosis is received, since until the grief is dealt with and some level of acceptance of the disability is achieved, the entire family system will suffer. Additionally, parents cannot help their special child grow to his or her full potential without first dealing with their own feelings. Information about the disability alone is not enough, although it is a start. Parents need to know that feelings of fear, guilt, anxiety, and pain are appropriate. They need to see disbelief and shock as normal responses to learning that a child has a disability and self-pity and mourning as appropriate responses to shattered dreams. They need to anticipate feelings of self-blame and guilt and accept feelings of shame surrounding disability as natural, normal, and even unavoidable in the context of our culture's preoccupation with perfection. They need to come to appreciate denial of pain and suffering as an automatic defense mechanism that acts as a buffer against shocking loss. And, of course, they need to be prepared, as much as possible, for the extraordinary claims that will be made upon their time and emotional resources, as well as for the inherent feelings of resentment and anger that accompany those claims. Until parents understand that these emotional responses are to be expected and are totally natural, the healing process will not begin.

It is imperative that parents of children with disabilities be given the opportunity to work with counselors in order to work through their grief. Parent support groups are also an effective way for parents to work through grief issues. When led by a professional or paraprofessional, support groups can provide a framework for mothers and fathers to understand the roller coaster of emotions they are experiencing. A group helps participants realize that they are not isolated and alone in their predicament. It also provides a means of learning how others are handling similar situations.

By facing and dealing with their grief, parents of children with special needs will get in touch with that place inside of themselves where deep pain can be a means of breaking through to new levels of love and acceptance. Many people avoid pain, and in so doing remain comfortable, yet stagnant. Parents of disabled children do not have this luxury. The pain is unavoidable as they care for their beloved child each day. Their choice is to acknowledge that pain and move past it, or remain mired within it. Pearl S. Buck writes of the hard-won wisdom she came to in her own journey as she moved toward acceptance of her daughter's disability.

> *They write to ask me what to do. When I answer I can only tell them what I have done. They ask two things of me: first, what they shall do for their children; and, second, how shall they bear the sorrow of having such a child? The first question I can answer, but the second is difficult indeed, for endurance of inescapable sorrow is something which has to be learned alone. And only to endure is not enough. Endurance can be a harsh and bitter root in one's life, bearing poisonous and gloomy fruit, destroying other lives. Endurance is only the beginning. There must be acceptance and the knowledge that sorrow fully accepted brings its own gifts. For there is an alchemy in sorrow. It can be transmuted into wisdom, which, if it does not bring joy, can yet bring happiness.* [6]

Notes
1. Barbara Gill, *Changed by a Child: Companion Notes for Parents of a Child with a Disability* (New York: Doubleday, 1997), 42.
2. Kathleen Deyer Bolduc, *His Name Is Joel: Searching for God in a Son's Disability* (Louisville, Ky.: Bridge Resources, 1999), 26.
3. Robert A. Naseef, *Special Children, Challenged Parents: The Struggles and Rewards of Parenting a Child with a Disability* (Secaucus, N.J.: Birch Lane Press, 1997), 35–36.
4. Beth Kephart, *A Slant of Sun: One Child's Courage* (New York: William Morrow, 1998), 54.
5. Gibran, *The Prophet*, 29.
6. Pearl S. Buck, *The Child Who Never Grew*, 2nd ed. (Bethesda, Md.: Woodbine House, 1992), 25.

The following poem chronicles my own journey from the bitter root of endurance to the flowering of acceptance.

Waiting Rooms

I spend so many hours
in waiting rooms
pediatrician, neurologist
behavioral specialist, psychiatrist
school psychologist, play therapist
so many doctors
so much advice
so little understanding
what do they know
despite diplomas
on waiting room walls
of living with disability?
It's different here
This therapist knows disability
It moved in twenty-some years ago
with her first-born child
She teaches my son how to play
leaving me alone
with a cup of tea, my thoughts, and magazines
Travel & Leisure, Smithsonian, Family Fun
Sometimes I read them and fume
What happened to my family's fun?
Only the beach for us
familiar and undemanding
No museums or theme parks
too stimulating
No long road trips stopping
at motels with pools each night
too disruptive

Above the magazine rack
brochures offer a better life
Women's Mind-Body Wellness,
Natural Wellness & Healing,
Conflict Management
I hear my son's laughter
the sound of knocking on flimsy walls
his current game, sometimes funny
more often annoying as hell

I sip raspberry tea
and step into Monet's garden
onto a bridge awash
in a dream of green
countless scenes of beauty
just outside the cottage door
waiting for the artist's brush

I wonder
Can I carve a garden
from the weedy turf of life
plant colors of my choosing
in arrangements pleasing to my eye
weed out thistles
of resentment and fear
replace them with flowers
of joy and contentment?

Suspended between past and future
in this waiting room
today
I weave a garden plan of beauty
while I wait
for my son

4 Disability and the Family System

Every child comes into a family somewhat like a rock thrown into a pond. The ripples caused by the new arrival affect everyone. Nobody in the family remains exactly the same. Everyone changes. When a youngster has a handicap, the family often expends energy beyond the ordinary. An increased sharpening of wits and widening of hearts become necessary so that the one with the handicap can be understood, loved, and accepted as a member of the close-knit family circle.[1]

One of Joel's favorite stores at our neighborhood mall overflows with all sorts of science paraphernalia: telescopes, magnets, rocks, and minerals. Even the upper atmosphere cries out for attention with graceful mobiles, suspended from the ceiling, moving in the breeze created by bodies moving through the store's space. Three-dimensional forms of sculpture with freely moving parts, they gently sway this way and that, constantly shifting to find that perfect balance.

A family system resembles a mobile. The members make up an interdependent system that is ever changing, yet maintains a certain balance. Each member of the family has his own place in the family hierarchy, as well as her own role to play, and family values and rules are implicitly understood. When sudden change occurs, such as the birth of a new child, disability, death, accident, loss of employment, or when the family moves into a new life stage, the mobile dances, attempting to maintain its equilibrium and find its former balance. It matters not whether the former state of equilibrium was functional or dysfunctional; the family will unconsciously try to return to what is known and comfortable and therefore safe.

Families of children with disabilities must deal not only with a unique set of problems as they attempt to adjust to meet the needs of their disabled child. They must also deal with the same problems and pressures facing any family. Will both husband and wife work outside the home? If so, who will provide child care and how will the household chores be divided? If not, who will stay home with the children and who will be the primary wage earner? What unwritten family rules will be established? How will conflict be negotiated? How will discipline be handled? What values will the family live by?

In a healthy, stable family, family roles are clearly defined, and rules are implicitly understood. There is little need for constant renegotiating. But even in the healthiest of families, when disability strikes, all the best laid plans come tumbling down. Rules and roles that were taken for granted just yesterday are called into question. A sudden and dramatic shift in the family structure takes place, having a profound impact on the family system. An irrevocable change occurs in the dreams for the future of both the child and the family, and a major role reorganization takes place as parents come to terms with the reality of prolonged care. In the following pages are described the major changes faced by families as they come to terms with a child's handicapping condition.

SITUATIONAL TASKS FACING THE FAMILY[2]

There are five situational tasks that face every family of a child with a disability.

1. *Obtaining and carrying out treatment.* This task varies depending on the age of the child when the disability is diagnosed. Some handicapping conditions, such as Down Syndrome and cerebral palsy, are detectable at birth. When this is the case, families are put into immediate contact with specialists, plugged into early intervention programs, and often directed to parent support groups. With other disabilities, such as autism, learning disabilities, or mild mental retardation, diagnosis can be elusive, and parents may spend a great deal of time and energy finding the right physician, clinic, or therapist. Some pediatricians advocate a "wait and see" philosophy when a child does not develop according to schedule, and parents lose precious time in locating services.

2. *Handling medical, financial, and transportation needs.* The demands of doctor and therapy visits can be overwhelming and frustrating, especially if there are other young children in the family, or if both mother and father work outside the home. For families that live in rural areas, specialists may be hours away, and weekly therapy an exercise in frustration. Some families uproot themselves for months at a time to visit a clinic or specialist in another part of the country. The financial burden of specialized care can be devastating to those families living with meager resources, and in some cases, little or no medical insurance.

3. *Coping with reactions and attitudes of significant others.* As parents struggle to come to terms with a child's disability, the way in which extended family members and friends react to

the child may be experienced as life-affirming or devastating. Those who accept and love the child unconditionally, while not denying the parents' grief, are life preservers in a temporarily stormy sea. Unfortunately, many people are uncomfortable with anything outside of their known realm of existence, and it is not unusual to find one's circle of friends slowly diminishing. Rejection of the child can feel like rejection of self. For a parent who is working through his or her own ambivalence toward a child whose disability has turned life upside down, the stares of strangers may be experienced as shaming.

4. *Altering lifestyle to accommodate needs and problems of the child.* Without a doubt, lifestyles have to change in some ways when a child with a disability enters the family system. Some disabilities require that one parent stay at home as caregiver because professional care is cost prohibitive. Others, such as autism, Attention Deficit Hyperactivity Disorder, and some forms of mental retardation, bring with them behaviors that make community outings difficult, and families find themselves isolated at home, giving up family vacations and outings with other children. If long-term specialized care is needed, rural families may find it necessary to move to the city. In some cases, families relocate to be nearer to, and receive support from, extended family.

5. *Insuring access to medical and community resources.* For those new to the disability community, especially in the beginning of the journey, ignorance of available resources may be a huge obstacle to moving forward. The importance of plugging families into the service delivery system cannot be overestimated. This is where doctors, counselors, school personnel, and church staff can be of indispensable help.

CHANGES IN PARENTAL ROLES

One of the first role reorganizations that occurs when disability enters the family system, either through a child's birth or through accident, is between husband and wife. Dynamics change dramatically as each partner scrambles to find his or her former balance in the system. The following characteristics have been noted in the husband/wife dynamic.

• Parental roles often become rigid and traditionally defined.

• Mothers tend to be more open with their emotions regarding their grief, whereas fathers tend to remain in denial for a longer period of time.

• In the majority of cases, the mother becomes the primary caregiver, with her life being defined by the child's needs. In this role, the mother can be overwhelmed with duties directly related to the disability. These might include nursing the child; visiting specialist after specialist; dispensing medications; taking the child to occupational, physical, and speech therapy; and visiting behavioral psychologists, as well as handling difficult behaviors at home. It is also extremely difficult to find child care for a child with special needs, and certainly cost prohibitive for many families. Federal law has mandated early intervention preschools for children with handicapping conditions, but for the first three years of the child's life the day-to-day responsibilities frequently rest mainly upon the mother's shoulders.

• Even when the child is in school, the amount of time needed for doctor and therapy visits often prohibits the mother from going back to work outside the home.

• Some research has shown that the family's reaction to the disabled child is directly dependent on the mother's attitude. If this is the case, it puts an enormous burden on the woman who is struggling to care for the often staggering needs of one child while attempting to keep the rest of the family healthy, happy, and intact.

• Other research shows that it is the father's response to the child's disability that sets the tone for the family.

• It is the norm for fathers of children with disabilities to fill the traditional role of father as provider and protector. The cultural image of man and father as powerful and in control is impossible to fulfill as the father of the disabled child realizes he has absolutely no control over his child's impairment. Subsequently, feelings of anger and frustration are common among fathers of children with special needs.

• For many men, letting go of dreams of lineage, ego fulfillment, and athletic and vocational achievement is extremely difficult and brings about a sense of depression and hopelessness.

• Because of the inordinate amount of time the wife (who is most often the primary caregiver) must spend with the child, she often has little time left over for her husband, which may cause jealousy and resentment.

• Communication problems often surface as the husband reverts to a "Mr. Fix-it" role, and comes home from work with platitudes and simple solutions for the difficulties his wife has faced in her long day as caregiver.

• It is not uncommon for parents of children with special needs to feel they lack control over the events of their lives. This lack of control may be related to their inability to work effectively with the child or to access community services. Not knowing what to do or where to turn is frustrating and affects feelings of competence, resulting in additional stress.

• Oftentimes, marital dissatisfaction is projected onto the disabled child. Rather than face the fact that they are not meeting one another's needs, the husband and wife may argue over the way the child's needs are (or are not) being met. As several studies suggest, "The role of divorce, marital disharmony, and desertions by husbands has been reported to be disproportionately high in marriages where there is a child or youth with an exceptionality."[3]

• One of the greatest difficulties confronted by parents of children with special needs is the ongoing nature of the disability, since continuous, long-term care puts an added stress not only on the husband and wife individually, but also on the marriage relationship, and the family in general.

• A child's disability has a way of making parents face their own vulnerabilities, since parents often see their children as a reflection of themselves.

• For the parent who has not accepted or dealt with his or her own limitations, the child's disability may bring to the surface feelings of unworthiness, hurt, and shame.

• Unresolved issues, or "unfinished business" from one's family of origin may surface under the stress of adjusting to a child's disability.

• For the parent who is not ready to deal with such issues, a defensive strategy such as the "blame game" may be used to keep uncomfortable feelings at bay.

IMPACT ON SIBLINGS

Brothers and sisters of children with special needs have a unique set of cares and concerns. Without information about the disability itself—what caused it, what the sibling's limitations will be, what the future will hold—they will be confused, bewildered, and even frightened. Because of the intensity of the needs of the brother or sister with a disability, siblings often wonder, "What is my place in this family? Am I as important as my brother? Does Mom love me as much as she loves my sister?" Siblings of children with disabilities experience a myriad of confusing feelings such as jealousy, pride, anger, resentment, love, embarrassment, and fear for the future. They need help working through these feelings.

• Siblings often feel neglected and helpless.

• Siblings feel isolated when they are excluded from information concerning the disability. Sometimes parents attempt to hide the fact of the disability from the siblings. Even

when done with good intentions, this will almost surely backfire. Giving siblings the facts in an age appropriate manner will help lead them from confusion and fear toward acceptance.

• Siblings may feel guilty that they were spared having a disability, or may feel that they somehow caused the disability.

• It is not uncommon for siblings to feel resentment and jealousy over the amount of time their parents, especially the primary caregiver, spends with the child who has a disability.

• Siblings often feel inordinate pressure to excel in school, athletics, or behavior in compensation for their disabled sibling's inability to do so—this, too, may cause resentment.

• As the parents adjust their roles, siblings also need to learn new roles within the system.

• Siblings will likely be expected to help out with the child with a disability, which also can lead to resentment, anger, and the feeling that "it isn't fair!"

• Siblings of exceptional children often worry about the future. What will their sibling do as an adult? Where will he or she live? Who will take care of him or her long-term and what will their own role be in that care?

• Siblings often express a great deal of pride in their disabled brother's or sister's accomplishments, noting the challenges and hurdles the child has had to overcome.

• Intense loyalty is not uncommon in brothers and sisters of challenged children.

• Siblings will often fight to defend their sibling from teasing, unfair treatment, or prejudice. It is helpful if they are given the language to explain their sibling's disability to friends and acquaintances.

LIFE-CYCLE STAGES AND DISABILITY

Each life-cycle stage of a child with disability brings with it unique challenges and tasks. Below are listed life-cycle stages and their primary tasks.[4]

Early Childhood: Ages birth–5

- Obtaining an accurate diagnosis
- Informing siblings and relatives
- Locating services
- Seeking to find meaning in the exceptionality
- Clarifying a personal ideology to guide decisions
- Addressing issues of stigma
- Identifying positive contributions of exceptionality

School Age: Ages 6–12

- Establishing routines to carry out family functions
- Adjusting emotionally to educational implications
- Clarifying issues of mainstreaming versus special education
- Participating in Individualized Education Plan (IEP) conferences
- Locating community resources
- Arranging for extracurricular activities

Adolescence: Ages 13–20

- Adjusting emotionally to possible chronicity of exceptionality
- Identifying issues of emerging sexuality
- Addressing possible peer isolation and rejection
- Planning for career/vocational development
- Arranging for leisure-time activities
- Dealing with physical and emotional changes of puberty
- Planning for postsecondary education

Adulthood: Ages 21 plus

- Planning for possible need for guardianship

- Addressing need for appropriate adult residence
- Adjusting emotionally to adult implication of dependency
- Addressing the need for socialization outside the home
- Initiating career choice or vocational program

POSITIVE CONTRIBUTIONS MADE TO THE FAMILY BY A CHILD WITH SPECIAL NEEDS

Children with disabilities bring many gifts to their families and communities. They model unconditional love; teach us how to live in the moment; bring joy, blessing, and fulfillment to those who accept them as they are; provide rich lessons in what it means to be human; make us realize how much we take for granted; give us new pride in small accomplishments; help us see the miracles in everyday life; and lead us to a deeper relationship with God. Read any of the literature written by parents of children with disabilities and you will soon learn that along with the struggles of raising these very special children come very real rewards. Consider the following selections.

In his strange, not-quite-human way, he is constantly reminding me that real magic doesn't come from achieving the perfect appearance, from being Cinderella at the ball with both glass slippers and a killer hairstyle. The real magic is in the pumpkin, in the mice, in the moonlight; not beyond ordinary life, but within it.[5]

Jessica has taught me what true love is. Poets and preachers, young lovers, and idealists have professed a knowledge of this elusive concept for years. But, in Jessica's silence, I have learned the real essence of love: you give everything and expect nothing in return. . . . The joy of loving her is its own reward. This could quite possibly be the purest love I've ever felt, untainted by worldly expectations, unaffected by demands, cause or effect. It simply surrounds you.[6]

The ten years of Walter's life have been ten years of the greatest love and joy imaginable. The love

I feel for Walter is so particular to him that it is impossible to imagine that same feeling for a "normal" Walter. I cannot imagine being as moved by the achievements of a typically developing child as I am with every small step Walter takes in his development. The road is not level for Walter. Every small step Walter takes is uphill.[7]

Maybe these are the lessons I am to learn from this child. How to be open and vulnerable. How to live in the moment. How to greet the day with simple joy.[8]

Ella provides joy beyond words. . . . She is a miracle in motion, a teacher and giver unaware, a constant reminder of a greater strength in the universe. She has been the innocent giver of a new kind of love, and a model of how the simple things in life can provide much contentment.[9]

Notes

1. Robert Perske, *Hope for the Families: New Directions for Parents of Persons with Retardation or Other Disabilities* (Nashville, Tenn.: Abingdon Press, 1973), 14.
2. Categories are from L. M. Fortier and R. L. Wanlass, "Family Crisis Following the Diagnosis of a Handicapped Child," *Family Relations* (January 1984): 22.
3. Ann P. Turnbull and H. Rutherford Turnbull III, *Families, Professionals, and Exceptionality,* 2nd ed. (Columbus, Ohio: Merrill, 1990), 56.
4. Adapted from Turnbull and Turnbull, *Families,* 134–135.
5. Martha Beck, *Expecting Adam: A True Story of Birth, Rebirth, and Everyday Magic* (New York: Random House, 1999), 73.
6. Donald J. Meyer, ed., *Uncommon Fathers: Reflections on Raising a Child with a Disability* (Bethesda, Md.: Woodbine House, 1995), 2.
7. Ibid., 76.
8. Bolduc, *His Name Is Joel,* 117.
9. Beth Gjerde, participant in a retreat for parents of children with disabilities led by author at Ghost Ranch, Abiquiu, New Mexico, July 2000.

For surely I know the plans I have for you, says the Lord, plans for your welfare and not for harm, to give you a future with hope. Then when you call upon me and come and pray to me, I will hear you. When you search for me, you will find me; if you seek me with all your heart, I will let you find me, says the Lord.

(Jer. 29:11–14a)

5 | What Then Shall We Do?

God has set each member of the body in the place God wanted it to be. If all the members were alike, where would the body be? There are, indeed, many different members, but one body. The eye cannot say to the hand, "I do not need you," any more than the head can say to the feet, "I do not need you." Even those members of the body which seem less important are in fact indispensable.

(1 Cor. 12:18–22, paraphrased)

It is my hope that the preceding pages will not only have piqued your interest, but will have convinced you of the need to consider families of children with disabilities in your ministry plans. Joel was on the precipice of adolescence when I began this project in 1997. Just twelve years earlier, before his birth and the advent of disability into our family life, I was oblivious to the needs, gifts, and desires of those living with disabling conditions. My journey with Joel has opened not only my eyes, but my heart as well. I have spent countless hours since then thinking and praying about the church's ministry to and with those who are disabled, as well as their families.

RESULTS OF PARENT SURVEY

I have also spent a great deal of time talking about this subject with friends who, like me, live with and/or love children with handicapping conditions. They are impassioned and articulate when asked how the body of Christ can (and all too often, doesn't) minister to and with them. In 1996, I conducted an informal survey via the Internet. I received thirty responses. Of these, fifteen indicated that they attend church regularly. Below is a breakdown of those responses.

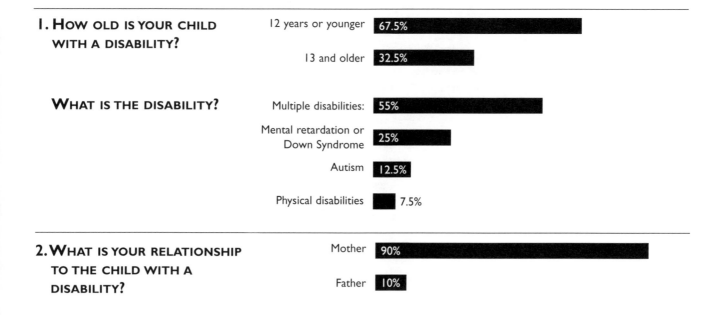

1. HOW OLD IS YOUR CHILD WITH A DISABILITY?

12 years or younger	67.5%
13 and older	32.5%

WHAT IS THE DISABILITY?

Multiple disabilities:	55%
Mental retardation or Down Syndrome	25%
Autism	12.5%
Physical disabilities	7.5%

2. WHAT IS YOUR RELATIONSHIP TO THE CHILD WITH A DISABILITY?

Mother	90%
Father	10%

3. IN WHAT WAYS HAS YOUR CHURCH BEEN HELPFUL TO YOU AS THE PARENT OR FAMILY MEMBER OF A CHILD WITH A DISABILITY?

Category	Percentage
Welcoming attitude	93.5%
Practical help	40%
Not at all helpful	30%
Support from pastoral staff	26.7%
Prayer support	13.3%
Acceptance	13.3%
Inclusion	13.3%
Support from other parents of children with special needs	10%
Accessibility	10%
Special classes	6.7%

4. IN WHAT WAYS HAS YOUR CHURCH NOT BEEN HELPFUL TO YOU AS THE PARENT OR FAMILY MEMBER OF A CHILD WITH A DISABILITY?

Category	Percentage
No special outreach to the child or family by pastoral or Christian education staff	53.3%
Church staff and members are not accepting of the child	40%
Building not accessible	16.7%
Not inclusive	16.7%
Condemnatory (disability is evidence of past sins or lack of faith)	13.3%
No support for parents' need to worship	10%
Child's gifts not recognized	6.7%
No problems	13.3%

5. IF YOU COULD CREATE YOUR "DREAM CHURCH," HOW WOULD THAT CHURCH MEET YOUR SPECIFIC NEEDS AS A PARENT OR FAMILY MEMBER OF A CHILD WITH A DISABILITY?

Category	Percentage
Welcoming attitude	76.7%
Trained staff	50%
Acceptance of the child's differences and limitations	40%
Inclusiveness	30%
Practical support	20%
Accessibility	16.7%
Disability education offered to congregation	26.7%
Recognition of child's gifts	13.3%
Pastoral support	6.7%

Note: Many of the respondents had tried several churches before settling into a church family. Therefore, percentages do not add up to 100%.

WHAT PARENTS DESIRE

What do parents of children with disabilities desire from their church communities? Their needs are not so different from those of any parents. They desire what most of us are looking for in a church community: acceptance, worship, fellowship and support, education, spiritual growth and discovery of giftedness, and friendship.

Acceptance

> [Allen] couldn't speak or move around on his own. He was tiny. Even at his death at age 14 he was only 36 inches long and 16 pounds. He was fed by a pump and gastronomy tube. He was catheterized. So many interventions, and so many things to intimidate the average person, but Allen was always loved and adored. He thrived on it, and I always called him the "honorary greeter" at church. His wheelchair sat at the end of a row of pews (a special place was saved for us every week by one of the ushers who wanted to make sure we never had to look for a place to sit). As people would file out at the end of the service, one by one they would say "Hi" to Allen, or kiss him, or pat him, and he sat there beaming and giggling.
>
> Survey respondent, mother of a child with a rare and fatal genetic disease (child's name was changed for publication)

Who among us does not long for a place that is safe; a place where we are welcomed with open arms; a place where we can take off our masks, be wholly ourselves, and still be accepted? Each of us longs for the unconditional love of Jesus Christ. The church, as the body of Christ, is the one place within this world we hope to find this kind of acceptance. Parents of children with special needs long for a church where their sons and daughters are loved and accepted just as they are. We live in a culture that worships physical beauty and judges a person's worth on what he or she produces or achieves. Our society often relegates persons with disabilities to a second-class citizenship, treating them with fear, pity, or condescension. Parents of children with disabilities long for a church that loves and

accepts their children regardless of appearance, behavior, or ability to achieve; a church that takes seriously Isaiah's plea to "enlarge the site of your tent, and let the curtains of your habitations be stretched out" (Isa. 54:2a).

> As many of you as were baptized into Christ have clothed yourselves with Christ. There is no longer Jew or Greek, there is no longer slave or free, there is no longer male or female; for all of you are one in Christ Jesus (Gal. 3:27–28).

Worship

> [Allen] died a year ago. . . He was 14 years old. . . . Our entire family attends church together . . . We made it a priority (and still do) to attend church together, no matter what else is going on, because our faith is the foundation of our life. We want our children to experience worship as a part of a congregation.
>
> Survey respondent, mother of a child with a rare and fatal genetic disease (child's name was changed for publication)

Most of us look forward to Sunday as a time to worship God as a community, to lift our voices together in praise, to enter into prayer individually and with a communal voice, to experience the presence of the Holy Spirit, to partake of the Lord's Supper, and to be spiritually fed so that we may be equipped to go out into the world as salt and light in the name of Jesus. All parents have the need to worship as community, especially parents whose children have physical or mental disabilities, as they face an ongoing struggle that calls on physical, emotional, and spiritual reserves. Some of us dream big, others dream small, and still others dream of what most people take for granted—the ability to get around a church campus.

Most parents assume that there will be child care for their babies, Sunday school for their children and teens, and that they (mom and dad) will be able to attend worship together. Unless the church staff is willing to accommodate the special needs of each child, parents of children with handicapping conditions lose the blessing of worshiping together as husband and wife, or as a family unit. In my own case, worshiping together is such a high priority that my husband and I will usually stay home rather than worship separately. As was pointed out in the previous chapter, marriages often suffer tremendous stress when parents care for a child with a disability. It is important to consider the revitalizing and rejuvenating role worship plays for these families.

> *O come, let us worship and bow down, let us kneel before the Lord, our Maker! For he is our God, and we are the people of his pasture, and the sheep of his hand (Ps. 95: 6–7a).*

Fellowship and Support

> *Mainly, the helpful things were the phone calls to check on us, the reminders that we were being prayed for, asking us how we were doing and listening—really listening to the answer—and above all, in the way people in our church loved Allen.*
>
> Survey respondent, mother of a child with a rare and fatal genetic disease (child's name was changed for publication)

As M. Scott Peck penned with such eloquent understatement, "Life is difficult."[1] Illness, injury, the death of loved ones, divorce, alcoholism, drug abuse, unplanned pregnancies, loss of jobs, disability, bankruptcy—difficulties are manifold and not one among us will go through life unscathed. We trust in our church communities to bear us up during the difficult portions of our journeys, providing practical support, prayer support, listening ears, shoulders to cry on, or perhaps just an affirming word. We also trust in our communities to share and celebrate the joys of our lives.

Community life is also filled with many joys. The familiar rhythm of the liturgical year, with its theme of birth, death, and rebirth, comforts us as we reexamine on a yearly basis the roots of our faith. As our roots deepen we develop wings of hope to carry us through harder times. As family, we celebrate the birth of each new child in our midst, and, as a church family, promise to help raise the child to know the story of our faith and to develop a personal relationship with Jesus Christ. Together, we celebrate graduations,

engagements, and marriage. We celebrate the birth of a new generation, as the circle of life continues unbroken.

Parenthood is perhaps the hardest job any of us will undertake, and disability makes it even more difficult. The pressures of frequent doctor and therapy visits, advocating for the child's rights in school, dealing with daily care at home, and handling difficult behaviors make the job of caregiving stressful for any parent, regardless of income, education, strength of character, or depth of faith. Such parents look to their church families for prayer support, help with child care, occasional meals, assistance with transportation when schedules become overwhelming, offers to include their children in church events, support groups within which they can share struggles and joys, and the simple reassurance that people care. They especially appreciate support from pastors and church staff. While counseling is sometimes needed and appreciated, it is amazing how encouraging a simple phone call and a "Hi, how are you all doing?" can be.

> *Bear one another's burdens, and in this way you will fulfill the law of Christ (Gal. 6:2).*

Education

> *Some of the research on inclusion shows that children without disabilities show greater compassion, less stereotypes, and even less fears about failure when in classrooms with children with disabilities. What better way to develop evangelical entrepreneurs than to have children learning from each other about perseverance, alternative methods of learning, and even coping with failure?*
>
> Survey respondent, father of a child who was born blind

Most of us come to church not only to worship God, but also to grow in knowledge of the Word of God. We look to the church for organized Bible studies and adult Christian education classes covering a variety of topics. We trust that the church will help us teach our children the story of our faith in the midst of the pressures of the increasing marginalization of the church in our society.

A Place Called Acceptance

We take it for granted that our churches will provide structured educational opportunities for our children. An often unfulfilled dream for parents of children with unique learning challenges is that their son or daughter will attend Sunday school with his or her peers. They long for a church where the Christian education staff not only welcomes their child, but is willing to make adaptations to ensure their son's or daughter's success. Not only do such parents want their child to learn the gospel, they want them to experience that learning in the context of community. Marilyn Bishop, former head of the Center for Ministry with Persons with Disabilities at the University of Dayton (Ohio), speaks to the blessings of inclusion: "Including children with special needs is a way of making all children feel accepted, valued, and welcomed in our church community. It's a way of teaching gospel love and forgiveness around people who are different, even as Jesus did."[2]

So faith comes from what is heard, and what is heard comes through the word of Christ (Rom. 10:17).

SPIRITUAL GROWTH AND DISCOVERY OF GIFTEDNESS

Please remind these pastors that our children aren't mistakes, just disabled in a temporary, worldly sense. We need opportunities for genuine friendship and support, not pity or condescension. Most of all, we need them to know that we have just as high expectations (albeit different) for our children as other parents, and want our children equipped to serve just like the others. . . Many members of the church reflect society's attitudes—that we are to be pitied, that Johnny can't do anything and must always be served. We routinely have to remind people that he is a little boy, not a diagnosis.

Survey respondent, father of a child who was born blind

Every one of us is gifted according to the grace of the Holy Spirit, regardless of intellectual or physical ability. Each of us longs to be of service to God, and we look to the church to help us discover our spiritual gifts. The prevailing cultural view is that people with disabilities are to be served, incapable of giving back to the community. All parents look to the church community to help discern and utilize their child's unique nature and gifts.

Stacey Schloss, a young woman who spends time on a weekly basis with our son Joel, speaks of the gifts he has bestowed upon her.

I first met Joel the summer after my junior year in college while pursuing a music therapy major. I was excited about working with him as we shared many common interests—music, nature, caring for animals—and I believed that spending time with him would help develop my skills for assisting people who have limited communication abilities and life skill functioning. However, I soon discovered that Joel had far more to teach me than specific skills, and the limitations we encountered were often not his, but my own. In the past year and a half, Joel has taught me to trust my intuition, to relinquish control in order to be fully present to him, and to not allow fear to prevent me from sharing my gifts. He has taught me that God, in his many voices, speaks to us if we have the courage to listen.

Some gifts that children with disabilities bring can only be brought by those who have a visible disability. Often, when we don't know what to say or do we avert our eyes and walk the other way. This is very common when we encounter persons with disabilities and their parents. Our own discomfort keeps us from reaching out. We need to learn that it is okay to be uncomfortable! One of the gifts people with disabilities bring to our church families is that they help nudge us out of our comfort zones. Once nudged, we are required to live by faith rather than by will. By accepting our powerlessness we release the power of God to work within us.

Now there are varieties of gifts, but the same Spirit; and there are varieties of services, but the same Lord; and there are varieties of activities, but it is the same God who activates all of them in everyone. To each is given the manifestation of the Spirit for the common good (1 Cor. 12:4–7).

Friendship

Friendships are such an everyday thing, we just take them for granted. They are like electricity, telephone, clothing, and three meals a day—we anguish only when we are deprived of them. And yet, we have just begun to sense the pain experienced by people with disabilities when they are deprived of mutually satisfying friendships with ordinary people. We suddenly see that family support, regular schooling, and community resources are not enough. Those people need friends just as we do.[3]

Once we are welcomed and accepted into a church family, we learn to trust our family members and risk revealing our deeper selves. This is the beginning of friendship, where we become brothers and sisters in Christ and where we develop deeply satisfying relationships. All parents desire that their children's lives be filled with friends. Because inclusion is the exception rather than the norm in many of our schools and communities, parents of exceptional children dream that their church community might be one place their children will experience the joys of friendship. Some parents feel stigmatized and different because of their child's disability. They, too, desire friendships within the church. They especially desire friendships with other families with whom they can socialize and celebrate and receive the extra support they might need.

This is my commandment, that you love one another as I have loved you. No one has greater love than this, to lay down one's life for one's friends (John 15:12–14).

MAKING YOUR CHURCH A PLACE CALLED ACCEPTANCE

Whoever welcomes you welcomes me, and whoever welcomes me welcomes the one who sent me (Matt. 10:40).

How do people who are the church become "a place called acceptance" for families of children with disabilities? How do we develop welcoming attitudes? What specific ministries

can we put into place as we seek to knock down barriers and reach out to everyone in our church families? Below are offered some practical suggestions for the church community, for individuals who make up the church, and for church leaders.

Communal Tasks

• Make a commitment to minister to and with families of children with disabilities!

• Consider forming a committee or task force on disability issues. Invite persons with disabilities as well as parents of children with special needs to serve with others who have a heart for disability concerns.

• Make accessibility a priority. Many church boards use "But no one in this congregation uses a wheelchair!" as an excuse not to address accessibility. Of course no one in an inaccessible church uses a wheelchair—they can't get in the door! (See *That All May Enter*, listed in Appendix 2.)

• Make sure families know that all children are welcome in worship, regardless of distracting noises or behavior that may be a part of their disability. The National Organization on Disability writes,

It is not wise to assume that a person will "get nothing" from attending services. Faith is not measured by how fast it develops, nor are we fully aware of the depth and breadth of what any one of us gains from worship. When we restrain someone with a developmental disability from participating, we may be more worried about our own potential "embarrassment" than we are concerned about his or her religious experience.[4]

• Train greeters and ushers in disability etiquette. (See Appendix 1.)

• Make it known, through your bulletin or newsletter, that someone on staff is available for counseling with those who live with disability. Many parents, especially in the early stages of grief, will not seek outside professional help, but may be open to talking to a pastor or another member of the church family.

• Recruit professionals (psychologists, social workers, special educations teachers, and so forth) in the congregation to serve as consultants and advocates to families of children with disabilities. Advertise their services.

• Encourage families with challenged children to take part in all areas of congregational life. Issue special invitations to church picnics, retreats, potluck dinners, and other events. Offer to help out with transportation or as a "big buddy" for a child whose disability makes relaxation difficult for the parents.

• Offer large-print bulletins and hearing devices in worship, and make them easily accessible.

Developing a Welcoming Attitude As Individuals

• Remember that welcoming attitudes are like the chicken pox—they're contagious!

• Greet children with disabilities in the same way you would greet any other children. Although they may be incapable of responding in typical fashion, they will feel welcomed by your greeting. Many people, when confronted by children who are physically or mentally "different," choose to remain in their comfort zone by utilizing avoidance behavior, or not knowing what to say, suppressing their desire to reach out. This sends a strong message—one that says, "I don't care enough to want to get to know you." A simple "Hi! How are you today?" is a good place to begin, and makes child and family feel welcome.

• Talk directly to the child rather than using the child's parent as a translator. If the child does not answer immediately, be patient. Get down on the child's level and establish eye contact. Repeat your statement or question if necessary. If the child responds and you cannot understand what is said, ask him or her to repeat it. Even if the conversation ends there, you have communicated that the child is important in your eyes.

• If you notice a family member struggling with a child (behaviorally or perhaps in getting a wheelchair in or out of a car), don't be afraid to ask if there is anything you can do to help. Respect their answer if no help is wanted.

• When a child with a disability behaves inappropriately, use as little fanfare as possible in your response. The more attention you pay to the behavior, the more you reinforce the very behavior you do not want. Attempt to redirect the child, changing activities if necessary. Common sense goes a long way in most instances. Treat the child lovingly yet firmly, respect boundaries of personal space, and avoid situations that are known to upset the child. Ask the child's parents what techniques they use in handling disruptive behaviors at home. They may have a behavior plan from school to share with you.

• Try to understand that the behavior is part of the disability, not a character flaw. Fear of unpredictable behaviors often keeps church members from reaching out with compassion to those who are disabled. Behavioral issues are fairly common with some handicapping conditions, such as autism, Tourette's syndrome, attention deficit disorder, mental illness, and fetal alcohol syndrome.

• Allow the children to do as much for themselves as possible. Sometimes it will take them longer to complete a certain task. Be patient. Be there to give assistance, but do not impose yourself unless needed.

• Use people-first language when talking about disabilities, e.g., "Joel has moderate mental retardation," not "Joel is mentally retarded," or, "There is a little boy with autism in my daughter's Sunday school class," not "There is an autistic boy in Jenny's Sunday school class." Remember, no one wants to be identified by their disability, anymore than any of us want to be identified by any one aspect of ourselves.

How would you like to be referred to as "that bald man who leads youth group," or "that overweight woman who sits next to me in worship?" Think about it!

Pastoral Care with Families of Children with Disabilities

• Make sure that those who are responsible for grief ministry in your church are aware that parents of children with disabilities go through a period of grieving similar to that experienced by parents who have lost their children to death. Many parents within congregations are grieving in silence. Suggested resources: *The Disabled and Their Parents: A Counseling Challenge* by Leo Buscaglia; *Special Children, Challenged Parents: The Struggles and Rewards of Raising a Child with a Disability* by Robert A. Naseef. (See Appendix 2.)

• Take an active interest in this family with disability. Arrange a pastoral visit to the family's home. Make phone calls on a regular basis just to see how things are going. Stay in touch.

• Once you have established a relationship, ask the parents to share with you the dreams they once had for this child. Allow them to talk of their struggles toward acceptance of the child's disability and to vent feelings of anger, fear, frustration, and guilt if necessary. Encourage them to find meaning in their situation. Pray with them that God may begin forming within their hearts and minds a new vision for this precious child.

• Arrange a meeting between the parents and a member of the congregation who is well versed in family systems to consider the following questions: How has the stress of caregiving changed the dynamics of the system? Can the mother find a slice of time each day to call her own? Do the siblings, in an age-appropriate way, help in caring for the child's needs? Are they expected to do too much? Too little? Is the father feeling helpless? If so, what new role could make him feel useful again?

• If there are people in the congregation who are familiar with the social service agencies within the community, ask them to contact the parents. Early integration into the social service system is an important step as parents learn to advocate for their child's best interests physically, mentally, socially, and emotionally.

• Suggest local support groups for Mom, Dad, and siblings. Literature in the field supports the fact that support groups of parents of like-handicapped children are extremely valuable in breaking down barriers of isolation and in helping parents and families work through their grief. They also provide an arena for problem solving and networking.

• One of the greatest gifts a congregation can give families is the gift of respite care. Respite is defined as a time of temporary relief from pain, work, or stress. Continuous, twenty-four-hour-a-day caregiving responsibilities take a toll physically, mentally, and spiritually if the caregivers are not afforded an occasional break. It is often difficult for parents of children with special needs to find baby-sitters. Some marriages crumble under the strain, and siblings can experience resentment from missing out on ordinary family outings, such as going shopping or out to eat. In some cases, the parents can train volunteers in how to work with their child's diverse needs. In other cases, more specialized training may be needed. Recommended resource: *Sharing Care: The Christian Ministry of Respite Care,* by Judith K. Murphy. (See Appendix 2.)

• Make deacons or Stephen's ministers aware of the practical support parents of children with disabilities desire but are sometimes afraid to ask for. (See "Results of Parent Survey," p. 21, for ideas.)

• Consider hooking up family-to-family teams that could support one another.

Ministry Suggestions for Christian Education Staff and Volunteers

Let the children come to me, and do not stop them; for it is to such as these that the kingdom of heaven belongs (Matt. 19:14).

• Train Sunday school teachers in inclusion so that children with physical and mental disabilities are not only accommodated but welcomed into the Sunday school program. (See Appendix 2 for resources.)

• Use a multisensory teaching approach when teaching children with disabilities. All children will benefit from a lesson that uses all five senses: kinesthetic, auditory, visual, olfactory, and gustatory. Suggested resource: *Multisensory Worship Ideas* by Margot Hausmann. (See Appendix 2.)

• Recruit and train volunteers (adults or teens) to be "special buddies" to children who need extra support in the Sunday school classroom. Some people mistakenly believe you must have special training to work with children with disabilities. While training would be a bonus, this simply isn't true. All that is truly necessary is flexibility, an open, nonjudgmental and prayerful attitude, patience, a love for children, and a conviction that Jesus calls us to share the gospel with all children.

• Consider holding workshops on disability issues on an occasional basis. Ask parents of children with special needs for input, or if they would be interested in leading a class on how to reach out to those who are disabled.

SIX SUGGESTIONS FOR A GOOD START

God arranged the members in the body, each one of them, as he chose. If all were a single member, where would the body be? As it is, there are many members, yet one body. The eye cannot say to the hand, "I have no need of you," nor again the head to the feet, "I have no need of you." On the contrary, the members of the body that seem to be weaker are indispensable (1 Cor. 12:18–22).

Perhaps you are feeling overwhelmed after reading through the ministry suggestions thus far. That is understandable. There is much to learn and much work to be done. The best thing to do when facing a daunting task is to start small. Here are six suggestions to get you going. The relationships formed and excitement generated by your decision to become "a place called acceptance" should provide more than enough steam to move ahead!

1. Keep the families who are struggling with disability on your church's intercessory prayer list. Prayer support is one of the greatest gifts a congregation can give. Let the families know you are praying for them.

2. Ask parents of challenged children to give personal testimony from the pulpit or within adult education classes on an occasional basis. The lessons they have learned in kingdom living will inspire the entire congregation.

3. Build up your church library. Educate your congregation on a range of aspects related to disability through readily available books, videos, and audiotapes. (See Appendix 2.)

4. Place at least one copy of Robert Perske's book *Hope for the Families: New Directions for Parents of Persons with Retardation or Other Disabilities* (see Appendix 2) in your church library. Share it with every family who has a child with a disability. This book is a treasure!

5.   Find ways children with disabilities can contribute in Sunday school or in worship. Perhaps they can help pass out bulletins, be responsible for getting the pastor a drink of water before the service, pass out papers in Sunday school, or clean up after class. Our son Joel recently began a volunteer job at our church one afternoon a week, emptying wastebaskets. He loves it! Children with disabilities thrive on being needed, as do all children.

6.   Participate in Disability Awareness Sundays. Once a year plan worship around the theme of disability. Ask members of the congregation who have disabilities, as well as those whose children have disabilities, to help plan the service. (See Appendix 2.) Distribute copies of Appendix 1: "General Disability Etiquette and Disability Awareness."

Notes
1. M. Scott Peck, *The Road Less Traveled* (New York: Simon and Schuster, 1978), 15.
2. Marilyn Bishop, *Welcome One, Welcome All* (Dayton, Ohio: Center for Ministry with Persons with Disabilities, University of Dayton, 1992), videocassette.
3. Robert Perske, *Circles of Friends* (Nashville, Tenn.: Abingdon Press, 1988), 12.
4. Ginny Thornburgh, ed., *That All May Worship: An Interfaith Welcome to People with Disabilities* (Washington, D.C.: National Organization on Disability, 1997), 29–30.

6 | Epilogue

It was Communion Sunday. Joel, then eleven, sat between his father and me. As usual, we sat in the front pew so that Joel wouldn't be able to kick the pews in front of us or reach forward and grab someone's hair. By trial and error we had found that with Dad to his right, Mom to his left, and empty space to the front, Joel could usually sit through half of the worship service.

We began bringing Joel to worship with us when he was five. Because of behavioral issues stemming from his disability, we had temporarily given up on Sunday school. Sunday school was too much like "real" school, a place where "keeping it together" is a real struggle. Because Joel loves music, and is enthralled by the choir, the beginning of the service is something he looks forward to. It took other members of the congregation a while to get used to Joel's spontaneity. He often stands up, pretend baton in hand, and imitates the choir director. During hymns he loves to sing along, usually (thank God) on tune, with a few words right, and always with a loud "Amen!" at the end, generally a few beats behind the rest of the congregation.

During the boring parts of the service (any part without music is boring as far as Joel is concerned), Joel twists and turns in the pew, stares at the people behind us, waves at the pastor, swings his feet, claps his hands or stomps his feet (he usually saves these last two for times of silent prayer), and at least once during every service says in a loud voice, "I have to go to the bathroom!" As you can imagine, worshiping with Joel is an interesting experience. It's not unlike sitting on the edge of your seat during an action movie when you're not quite sure what's going to happen next, you only know something is going to happen. It's difficult to develop a prayerful attitude in those circumstances.

On the first Sunday of the month at our church, Communion is served. We pass the bread along the pews, administering it to one another, saying, "This is the body of Jesus, broken for you." Likewise, we pass the wine to one another with the words, "This is Jesus' blood, shed that you might live." My husband and I allow Joel to take a piece of bread, reciting the familiar words to which he never seems to pay attention. He chews the bread, picking at the sticky stuff left in his teeth with his fingers, but far prefers the wine, which in our church is really grape juice. Again, we recite the words to him. "Joel, this is Jesus' blood, shed for you." He slurps down the juice and sticks his tongue into the cup, determined to get every last drop. His father and I close our eyes briefly to pray our own private prayers of thanksgiving for this unbelievable gift of grace. Joel cranes his neck to watch as everyone else is served, and wiggles through the remaining quiet time.

This particular Sunday, the pastor raised the plate high in the air and proclaimed, "This is the body of Christ, broken for you." Then he raised the cup, saying, "And this is the blood of Christ, poured out that you might live." Joel pulled on my sleeve. I looked down to see him grinning, his face lit up as if from within. He stood up tall, and tapped himself on his chest. "For me! For me!" he cried joyfully. He turned around to the people behind us. "For me!" he repeated. "For me!"

Ordinary time stopped. All that existed in that moment was the radiant look of understanding on Joel's face. Joel knew that God loved him. On a spiritual level he knew that God had sent Jesus for him. My body remained in the front pew of College Hill Presbyterian Church, but my spirit stood in the sacred presence of God. All the accumulated Sunday hours of embarrassment, impatience, frustration, and yearning for wholeness as the world knows wholeness sloughed away as I watched the love of God glimmer like gold in the face of my son.

In 1 Cor. 13, Paul writes, "For now we see in a mirror dimly, but then face to face. Now I know in part; then I shall understand fully, even as I have been fully understood." For a moment the mirror of existence, like a mirror wiped clear of steam by a towel, brightened and cleared and I understood clearly. Joel, although cognitively impaired, is spiritually whole.

The sacred surrounds us as does the very air we breathe—an entire realm as real as this world we live in, but invisible to the naked eye. A realm beyond our concept of space and time. A realm where schedules and priorities and developmental timetables do not exist. A realm where it is enough simply "to be."[1]

Note
1. This story has appeared in the *Cincinnati Enquirer*, May 19, 1997, and *Family Ministry: Empowering Through Faith*, Winter 2000.

A Place Called Acceptance

Appendix 1

General Disability Etiquette and Disability Awareness

These pages may be photocopied for use on Disability Sundays or in disability training within the congregation.

GENERAL DISABILITY ETIQUETTE

- View the child with a disability as a person, not a disability.

- Do not condescend or patronize.

- Be courteous.

- Offer assistance, but ask before acting.

- When it is obvious, accept the fact that a disability exists (don't pretend otherwise).

- Speak directly to a child with a handicapping condition, not to an adult or sibling who is with the child. To ignore a child because of the presence of a disability is insensitive. To ignore a child in a group is rude.

- React to and treat children with disabilities as if they are healthy. Disability does not mean illness.

- Do not judge lack of a response from a child with a disability as rudeness. Disability may affect social or motor skills.

- Take care not to startle the child, e.g., coming up from behind, suddenly putting your face in the child's, or grabbing abruptly.

- Relax and enjoy the child!

DISABILITY AWARENESS: BLINDNESS

- Identify yourself when you greet the child.

- Never leave a blind child alone in an open area. Guide the child to a physical point of reference.

- Never leave a blind child alone without saying that you are leaving.

- Offer assistance to guide, if necessary, by offering your arm.

- Give verbal cues (such as, "We're coming to some steps").

- Describe your setting (colors, number of people, what people look like, ages).

- Use a normal voice—don't shout!

- Invite the child to join group conversation.

- Provide large print for visually impaired children.

- Be specific and clear when giving directions.

DISABILITY AWARENESS: MOBILITY IMPAIRMENT

- Speak directly to a child in a wheelchair, not to the parent or companion.

- Get down to eye level.

- Involve the child in conversation.

- Ask if the child needs assistance before offering it.

- Do not lean on a wheelchair or allow other children to hang or lean on a wheelchair.

- Do not use the phrase "wheelchair bound." For the people who use them, wheelchairs offer freedom, not imprisonment!

DISABILITY AWARENESS: SPEECH IMPAIRMENT

- Focus your whole attention on the child.

- Be patient. Let the child finish his or her sentences—don't jump in and finish sentences.

- Don't act frustrated or angry. If the child could speak more clearly, he or she would.

- Don't pass judgment on the child or parents. Speaking clearly is not a matter of will, and talking "baby talk" to young children is not the cause of speech impairment.

- Don't pretend to understand. Ask the child to repeat, if necessary. If you still don't understand, ask the child to say it another way or with gestures.

- Do not raise your voice or shout.

DISABILITY AWARENESS: MENTAL RETARDATION

- Greet the child normally.

- Interact naturally.

- Treat the child age appropriately.

- Treat the child the same as you treat the child's peers.

- Speak simply. Avoid complex sentences.

- Keep instructions simple, clear, and concise.

- Include the child in all activities, offering the opportunity to do anything the other children are doing.

- Remember children will receive more information than they will express. Don't underestimate how much information they are taking in, not only from your conversations with them, but from your conversations with others.

- Make sure someone sits next to the child in group settings, to convey acceptance.

- Enjoy the child's spontaneity as a gift in our up-tight world!

- Be patient. Children with mental retardation and other developmental disabilities may react to situations in an inappropriate manner.

DISABILITY AWARENESS: DEAFNESS AND HEARING IMPAIRMENT

- When speaking, position yourself where the child can see your face and mouth clearly.

- Speak clearly, distinctly, and at normal speed without exaggerated mouth movements.

- Use gestures and facial expression when speaking.

- Maintain eye contact during conversation.

- To get the child's attention, gently wave your hand or touch the child's arm.

- Don't assume comprehension—ask for feedback.

- Move closer rather than shouting to be heard.

- Turn off radio, television, air conditioner, or any distracting background noise.

- Learn American Sign Language, but do not assume all children with profound hearing loss know it—some schools of thought still discourage signing. Check with parents before signing to the child.

Appendix 2

Resources

ORGANIZATIONS

American Association on Mental Retardation
(AAMR) Religion Division
Bill Gaventa, Executive Secretary
gaventwi@umdnj.edu
(732) 235-4408
The Religion Division of the AAMR is an
interfaith association of professional ordained
and lay people who journey with persons with
developmental disabilities and their families.
They provide an invaluable resource for churches
and families entitled *Dimensions of Faith* and
*Congregational Ministries with Persons with
Developmental Disabilities and Their Families: A
Bibliography and Address Listing of Resources for
Clergy, Laypersons, Families and Service Providers.*

Bethesda Lutheran Home
700 Hoffmann Drive
Watertown, WI 53094
(414) 261-3050
Produces films, videotapes, and printed
materials relating to special education. Also,
available free on loan, videos and resources on
how to include people with mental retardation in
church life.

Christian Council on Persons with Disabilities
7120 W. Dove Court
Milwaukee, WI 53223
(414) 357-6672
Network of evangelical Christian denominations,
organizations, and individuals.

The Christian Church Foundation for the
Handicapped
PO Box 9869
Knoxville, TN 37940

Concordia Publishing House
3558 So. Jefferson Avenue
St. Louis, MO 63118
(314) 268-1000
Produces Sunday school curriculum for special
education.

Friendship Foundation
2850 Kalamazoo Avenue, SE
Grand Rapids, MI 49560
(616) 246-0842
Produces "Friendship Series" religious
curriculum for persons with cognitive
impairments.

Grace Community Church
13248 Roscoe Boulevard
Sun Valley, CA 91352
800-GRACE15
Produces teacher training curriculum.

The Healing Community
521 Harrison Avenue
Claremont, CA 91711
Dr. Harold Wilke
(909) 621-6808
Produces resources on accessibility, worship,
congregational ministry.

Home Mission Board
Church and Community Ministries Department
4200 N. Point Parkway
Alpharetta, GA 30202
Offers videos, brochures, information packets,
and much more to address disability awareness
in your church.

JAF Ministries
PO Box 3333
Agoura Hills, CA 91301
(818) 707-5664
Founded by Joni Eareckson Tada. Materials for
Disability Awareness Sunday; Bible study
material on disability awareness; family retreats.

National Alliance for the Mentally Ill (NAMI)
200 N. Glebe Road, Suite 1015
Arlington, VA 22203-3754
(800) 950-6264
(703) 516-7991 (TDD)

National Apostolate for Inclusion Ministry
PO Box 218
Riverdale, MD 20738
(800) 736-1280
www.nafim.org

National Catholic Office for Persons with
Disabilities
PO Box 29113
Washington, DC 20017
(202) 529-2933 (V/TDD)

National Council of Churches Division of
Education and Ministry
Committee on Disabilities
475 Riverside Drive
New York, NY 10115
(212) 229-4325

National Organization on Disability
910 Sixteenth Street NW
Suite 600
Washington, DC 20006
(202) 293-5960
(202) 293-5968 (TDD)
www.nod.org

NICE (Network for Inclusive Catholic Education)
Institute for Pastoral Initiatives, University of
Dayton
300 College Park
Dayton, OH 45469-0314
(937) 229-4356
www.udayton.edu/~ipi
A wealth of resources on including persons with
disabilities in the life of the church. Videos may
be rented or purchased. Curriculum and books
on lesson planning available.

PHEWA, Presbyterian Church (U.S.A.)
100 Witherspoon Street
Louisville, Ky. 40202-1396
(888) 728-7228, ext. 5794
This office coordinates a national Presbyterian
network in disability issues.

Southern Baptist Convention
127 N. Ninth Avenue
Nashville, Tenn. 37234
(800) 458-2772
Special education resource kit and Bible study.

MATERIALS

Adam: God's Beloved. Henri J. Nouwen.
Maryknoll, N.Y.: Orbis Books, 1997.

*After Your Child's Diagnosis: A Practical Guide for
Families Raising Children with Disabilities.* Cathy
Lynn Binstock. Manassas: E.M. Press, 1997.

*Agenda for Real Life: A Blueprint for Daily Living
Programs in Our Communities.* Sarah E. Eastes.
Louisville, Ky.: Advocado Press, 1994. Available
from Congregational Ministries Publishing,
PC(USA), Louisville, Ky., (800) 524-2612,
PDS 094010.

All God's Children: Ministry with Disabled Persons.
Joni Eareckson Tada and Gene Newman. Grand
Rapids: Zondervan Publishing House, 1993.
Becoming Human. Jean Vanier. Mahwah, N.J.:
Paulist Press, 1998.

The Broken Body. Jean Vanier. Mahwah, N.J.:
Paulist Press, 1988.

*Changed by a Child: Companion Notes for Parents of
a Child with a Disability.* Barbara Gill. New York:
Doubleday, 1997.

The Church and Disabled Persons. Griff Hogan, ed.
Springfield, Ill.: Templegate Publishers, 1983.

Circles of Friends: People with Disabilities and Their Friends Enrich the Lives of One Another. Robert Perske. Nashville, Tenn.: Abingdon Press, 1990.

Dancing with Disabilities: Opening the Church to All God's Children. Brett Webb-Mitchell. Cleveland: United Church Press, 1996.

Differences in Common: Straight Talk on Mental Retardation, Down Syndrome, and Life. Marilyn Trainer. Bethesda, Md.: Woodbine House, 1991.
The Disabled God: Toward a Liberatory Theology of Disability. Nancy Eiesland. Nashville, Tenn.: Abingdon Press, 1994.

Different Members, One Body: Welcoming the Diversity of Abilities in God's Family. Sharon Kutz-Mellem, ed. Louisville, Ky.: Bridge Resources, 1999.

The Disabled and Their Parents: A Counseling Challenge. Leo Buscaglia. Thorofare, N.J.: SLACK, 1994.

Discipline with Dignity. Richard L. Curwin and Allen Mendler. Alexandria, Va.: Association for Supervision and Curriculum Development, 1988.

Enough Room for Joy: The Story of L'Arche, A Message for Our Time. Bill Clarke. Mahwah, N.J.: Paulist Press, 1974.

Exceptional Parent. PO Box 3000, Dept. EP, Denville, N.J. 07834.

Fathers of Children with Special Needs: New Horizons. James May. Bethesda, Md.: Association for the Care of Children's Health, 1991.

God Plays Piano, Too: The Spiritual Lives of Disabled Children. Brett Webb-Mitchell. New York: Crossroad, 1993.

His Name Is Joel: Searching for God in a Son's Disability. Kathleen Deyer Bolduc. Louisville, Ky.: Bridge Resources, 1999.

Hope for the Families: New Directions for Parents of Persons with Retardation or Other Disabilities. Robert Perske. Nashville, Tenn.: Abingdon Press, 1973.
How to Reach and Teach All Students in the Inclusive Classroom. Sandra F. Rief and Julie A. Heimburge. West Nyack, N.Y.: Center for Applied Research in Education, 1996.

Human Disability and the Service of God: Reassessing Religious Practice. Nancy Eiesland and Donald E. Saliers, ed. Nashville, Tenn.: Abingdon Press, 1998.

It Isn't Fair! Siblings of Children with Disabilities. Stanley Klein and Maxwell Schleifer, ed. Westport, Conn.: Bergin and Garvey, 1993.

Life As We Know It: A Father, a Family, and an Exceptional Child. Michael Berube. New York: Vintage Books, Random House, 1996.

Living with a Brother or Sister with Special Needs: A Book for Sibs. Donald Meyer and Patricia Vadasy. Seattle: University of Washington Press, 1996.

Making Changes: Family Voices on Living with Disabilities. Jan Spiegel and Richard Van Den Pol, ed. Cambridge, Mass.: Brookline Books, 1993.

Multisensory Worship Ideas. Margot Hausmann. Available from Eastern Christian Children's Retreat, 700 Mountain Ave., Wyckoff, N.J. O7481. Please enclose a self-addressed stamped envelope.

NICE Inclusion Quarterly
Network of Inclusive Catholic Educators
Institute for Pastoral Initiatives, University of Dayton, 300 College Park Drive, Dayton, Oh. 45469-0317; (937) 229-4325
A quarterly newsletter covering issues including the theological rationale for inclusion, personal testimonies, and suggestions on how to make inclusion work in your church.

New Life in the Neighborhood: How Persons with Retardation or Other Disabilities Can Help Make a Good Community Better. Robert Perske. Nashville, Tenn.: Abingdon Press, 1989.

No Disabled Souls: How to Welcome People with Disabilities into Your Life and Your Church. Jim Pierson. Cincinnati: Standard Publishing, 1998. A good resource for churches starting a ministry for persons with disabilities.

Nobody's Perfect: Living and Growing with Children Who Have Special Needs. Nancy B. Miller. Baltimore: Paul H. Brooks Publishing, 1994.

Parenting Your Disabled Child. Bernard Ikeler. Philadelphia: Westminster Press, 1986.

The Power of the Powerless. Christopher de Vinck. Grand Rapids, Mich.: Zondervan, 1995.

Religion and Disability: Essays in Scripture, Theology, and Ethics. Marilyn E. Bishop, ed. Kansas City, Mo.: Sheed and Ward, 1995.

The Road to Daybreak: A Spiritual Journey. Henri J. Nouwen. New York: Doubleday, 1988.

Sharing Care: The Christian Ministry of Respite Care. Judith K. Murphy. New York: United Church Press, 1986.

And Show Steadfast Love. Lewis H. Merrick, ed. Louisville, Ky.: Presbyterian Church (U.S.A.), 1993.

A Slant of Sun: One Child's Courage. Beth Kephart. New York: William Morrow, 1998.

Special Children, Challenged Parents: The Struggles and Rewards of Raising a Child with a Disability. Robert A. Naseef. Secaucus, N.J.: Carol Publishing, 1997.

Strong at the Broken Places: Persons with Disabilities and the Church. Steward Govig. Louisville, Ky.: Westminster John Knox, 1989.

That All May Enter: Responding to People with Disability Concerns. Louisville, Ky.: Office of the General Assembly and the Education and Congregational Nurture Ministry Unit, Presbyterian Church (U.S.A.), 1989.

That All May Worship: An Interfaith Welcome to Persons with Disabilities. National Organization on Disability, 901 16th Street NW, Suite 600, Washington, D.C. 20006 (202) 293-5960, (202) 293-5968 (TDD)

That's My Child: Strategies for Parents of Children with Disabilities. Lizanne Capper. Washington, D.C.: Child Welfare League of America, 1996.

Tough to Reach, Tough to Teach: Students with Behavior Problems. Sylvia Rockwell. Reston, Va.: The Council for Exceptional Children, 1993.

Uncommon Fathers: Reflections on Raising a Child with a Disability. Donald J. Meyer, ed. Bethesda, Md.: Woodbine House, 1995.

Unexpected Guests at God's Banquet: Welcoming People with Disabilities into the Church. Brett Webb-Mitchell. New York: Crossroad, 1994.

NOTES

NOTES

NOTES